PIPERS CORNER
NT

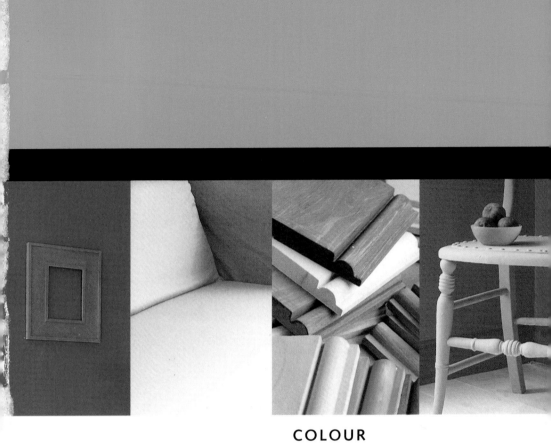

COLOUR

C O L

Original photography by
Marie-Louise Avery and Sue Baker

JOCASTA INNES AROUND THE HOUSE

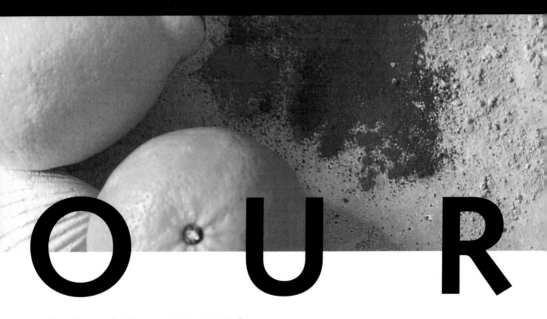

O U R

JOCASTA INNES

MACMILLAN

AROUND THE HOUSE is intended as a series that will expand into a whole shelf of stylish, practical and focussed handbooks for home decorators. Small enough to be affordable, but long enough to deal with their subjects in depth, they will offer a generous choice of hands-on projects, clearly explained and amplified by excellent, specially-commissioned photographs. If cooks can buy small, subject-specific books such as Pasta, Soups and Salads, why shouldn't decorators be offered the same approach, and choice? I believe this series – something of a publishing 'first' – will encourage a radical re-think of decorating books, their treatment, format and presentation.

Watch this space!

CONTENTS

INTRODUCTION

COLOUR IS THE HOME DECORATOR'S

RICHEST RESOURCE, also the cheapest, quickest and most versatile. Yet I know from experience, teaching, lecturing and running a decorating problem page, that for every person who feels comfortable with it there are at least ten who find putting colours together successfully in a room scheme a perplexing, intimidating — even scary — business. They collect swatches of paint and wallpaper, snippets of fabrics and carpet, tear-outs from magazines and spend anxious hours trying to decide whether this green in the curtain fabric is an exact match for the green sofa cover, whether a greige or beige carpet 'goes' best with other colours in a room, or whether pale blue walls will make it look chilly. Often, in desperation, they play safe by picking nondescript colours — then wonder why the result is disappointing, so far removed from the inviting image at the back of their minds.

I sympathize. Confidence in handling colour comes with practice and experience, which the average home decorator, tackling a room every three to five years, just doesn't get enough of. The colour chips and swatches handed out by fabric stores and paint companies are too small to be useful in 'visualizing'. Mistakes can be expensive, especially when it comes to soft furnishings, curtains, carpets, loose covers, upholstery. Those glossy magazine tear-outs which provide 'inspiration' can be misleading because clever photographic lighting and filters, not to mention adept styling, conspire to flatter a room scheme and add what it may lack — atmosphere, colour, charm, spaciousness.

But while I understand why so many people agonize about getting colours 'right', I also know that this approach is self-defeating. The more uptight you become when dealing with colour, the less chance you have of finding the best solution. Odd though it may seem, the proper way to approach it is playfully. Children often combine colours brilliantly because it doesn't occur to them to worry about whether this 'goes' with that. They just find them enjoyable and satisfying and play with pens, crayons or paint, gleefully but absorbedly. What psychologists call 'serious play' is increasingly recognized as a mainspring of creativity in all the visual arts. And choosing colours that work together in a room is certainly a form of creativity. So the big question is: how does a home decorator go from fussing and fretting to the seriously playful state in which choices seem to resolve themselves, and one happy inspiration somehow leads inevitably to many more?

R E L A X

■ Start with the wall colour. This is the determining factor in a room scheme. Get that right and the rest falls into place. Paint is cheap and reversible and this book shows umpteen ways to modify, remedy, soften or enrich colours that don't hit the mark.

■ Keep your options open. Don't rush out and pick all the fabrics in one go. Take a step at a time and live with your first decision before moving on to the next. Colours can affect each other in unexpected ways, so keep an open mind and a vigilant eye.

■ Forget itsy-bitsy samples and swatches. Only a trained eye can build confidently on these. Most paint companies sell sample pots. Paint big sheets of paper with your chosen colours, tape them up and consider their impact in different lights, moods, weather. Work towards fabric decisions using whatever comes to hand as props — clothes, cushions, remnants — before committing yourself. Lay them out, move them around in the room, gauge how they work with what you already have.

■ Remember that proportion — how much of a certain colour you build into the equation — is critical. A vivid blue chair could look stunning and right; vivid blue floor-length curtains might be just too much.

■ Sign on for a decorative painting course. It is astonishing how readily students acquire confidence, even on a one-day course; and the 'play-school' situation, gossiping as you mix and combine colours and effects and observe what everyone else does with their 'project', is relaxing and helpful.

■ Read this book, and study the pictures.

To give colour — funky, muted or barely there — its proper liberating role in your decorating plans, you must be ready to make mistakes. Everyone who works with colour agrees that mistakes teach you more than 'play safe' schemes. We show ways you may not have thought of to remedy disastrous colours. Repainting is the worst thing that can happen where a paint colour is the problem. But you need to go more cautiously with furniture, soft furnishings, carpets, tiles, etc., all of which represent a much larger investment — and one which you will have to live with.

In this book I have tried to give practical advice on handling colour combinations successfully in interior decoration, through paint in particular, without giving too much space to colour theory on the one hand, or lavish 'inspirational' room shots on the other. Although some understanding of primary, secondary and complementary colours can have a bearing on decoration, theoretical considerations are chiefly useful to artists, who must explore the interaction of colour all their lives. Recognizing undertones (so that you can tell a blue-red from an orange-red), using complementary colours to soften without 'dirtying', seeing how mixtures of white or black 'shade' a colour towards light or dark, gauging the subtlety of transparent overlays of colour — all these are immediately valuable in decorating, whereas understanding Newton's discovery that white light contains all the spectrum colours is probably academic. Inspirational pictures can ginger up your decorating thoughts, rather as recipes can enliven your cooking, but only when you learn to analyse them to see what makes them work visually and whether this applies to your own situation. It is no good falling for the feel-good factor in a Mediterranean-type colour scheme if you are stuck with dusty pink carpet and pretty-pretty flowered chintz.

It all starts, really, with intelligent looking rather than with a bunch of rules — especially since rules, when it comes to combining colours, clamour to be broken. When a particular combination stops you in your tracks don't just say, 'Hey, that's gorgeous!'. Pause to think about *why* it's gorgeous and why you love it. Is it the choice of colours, their intensity or otherwise, the balance achieved between them, a lot of white surrounding them, or the texture of the material (print fabric, weather-beaten stucco, faded needlepoint, flower arrangement, modern glass) that carries them along and makes them sing?

Like most decorators, or indeed artists, I tend to work from instinct. I get the basic colour scheme together first, and then cast about trying this or that contrast or texture until it 'clicks'. Experience has shown me that some colours just don't click. Work within a particular 'family' or palette and you can't go far wrong, but pile in a colour of a different family or vibrancy, as we do in our little cushion game on page 14, and the whole thing falls apart. However, some bright colour — a modern painting, kilim rug or a pot of geraniums — will look splendid against a neutral background (see page 63).

Once you have established your colour family, on walls and soft furnishings, the final challenge is to put your own spin on it, adding or subtracting this and that — and playing safe cost-wise to start with, until you find the colours that are needed, in the right proportions, to bring it all to life.

A REAL-LIFE COLOUR PROBLEM

This was sent in by a reader of the monthly decorating problem page I write for and I thought it was worth featuring because it illustrates one of the common mistakes people make when dealing with colour in a room scheme. She had spent time, money and, clearly, much thought selecting different fabrics — a check, a subdued floral and a vivid though washy pinky red print for upholstery, loose covers and curtains — all working around the same shade of pinky red. These had all been completed, installed and hung. But, she said sadly, the room looked 'horrendous', not how she had visualized it, not at all 'together'. What wall colour, she asked, would restore harmony and make these discordant and disparate elements work?

My first reaction was that she had put the cart before the horse in committing so much care and cash to easily variable elements like soft furnishings, instead of starting with a clear colour decision for the walls. Walls establish a room scheme for the obvious reason that theirs is the greatest area. Her next mistake was to have chosen the vivid red-on-pink print for her curtains. Such large slabs of strong colour would be certain to 'jump out' against pale walls and overwhelm the other fabrics. I would have chosen the check or subdued floral, both of which have a lot of white in them, for the curtains and used the red print on the sofa. In my experience, people worry endlessly about matching up colours in fabrics and trimmings without trying to 'visualize' how they will behave in context. If she had draped her red print over a window before getting it run up into curtains she would have realized that it had an unbalancing effect. Of course,

doing this is easier for professional decorators, who have bolts of fabrics to play around with before making these decisions.

The only possible solution was to paint the walls a colour strong enough to put the curtains in their place. The alternatives I suggested are shown above. A dark green, complementary to red, that picked up the green in her other fabrics was one possibility. An opaque red with a crimson cast (that is, an emulsion paint) was another. But these are relatively radical solutions and could seem overwhelming. Which left a further option: putting a pinky red glaze, or wash, over a pink base to give a softer wall colour almost identical to the overall tone of her curtain fabric. I felt this would 'lose' the curtains in a general rosiness, while pulling the whole scheme together, and the transparency of the wall finish would make its colour less assertive and enclosing.

The moral of this tale is to keep open as many options as you can when fixing up a room. Pin up fabric swatches (as large as possible — many decorators will lend these for a deposit) or lay them over the furniture to get an idea of their impact. If you don't fancy strongly coloured walls, pick a quiet print for curtains, with a lot of pale background colour so they blend in with pale walls. Try to visualize the effect of a fabric, especially a print, as a whole rather than from a tiny piece: in the store, drape it across the counter, stand back and look at it with half-closed eyes. You may find it 'reads' rather differently with one element dominating unexpectedly. And when in doubt, take wall colour as your starting-point; paint is so much less expensive than fabric that you could even afford to change your mind, whereas the wrong-coloured sofa or curtains are a costly and exasperating commitment.

A LITTLE COLOUR EXERCISE

This colour playlet shown overleaf took place in an area of my business's head office known as the 'meeting room', and backtracks on the process that led to the choice of certain soft furnishing colours. I hope that seeing how we made our final selection will throw up points that may be useful when you are working with colours.

The given colours to start with were a deep, moody blue-green on the walls (dark green colourwash on a pale green base) and the same green, offset against off-white, for the painted chequerboard floor. Lit by large, metal-framed, industrial-type windows at both ends, the effect was strong and clear — but sombre, especially on grey days. Two job-lot sofas, squashy foam in dark grey covers, turned sombre into mournful, sheerly by their dark presence. Shopping hastily, I picked a sunny, muted orange for sofa covers, which at once brought a feel of sunshine and warmth into the space. However, although the effect was an improvement, it was a one-liner in colour terms. It had impact but lacked subtlety and balance. It left me,

and other colour freaks, dissatisfied. The next step was to try out two cushions in a deeper, burnt orange against the sofa colour — the obvious progression if you are playing safe. You might add a cream cushion for lightness. But even so, the palette lacked surprise, a spark of the not-so-obvious, even a hint of 'clash'. These came when we added a pair of cushions in not-so-obvious shades: sugar pink, aqua blue. When slightly out-of-kilter colours, in measured doses, are mixed in with obviously harmonizing ones, a visual tension, lively without being discordant, is set up. It has a 'wake-up' effect all-round that is out of proportion to its area. It is one of the fun games you can play in decoration, at no great cost but with real impact.

However, colour anarchy can go so far that it defeats itself. You may, if you are a colourist by nature, have spotted that all the colours used so far belonged, loosely, to a family: chalky brights and pastels of roughly similar intensity. Bring in a serious 'bright' of a wholly different intensity of hue, like the magenta napkin we finally laid across our cushions, and the result is a rout. The chalky colours, deliciously contrasting before, look wiped out, while the vivid magenta is visibly not at home — a lone wolf looking for a bright scene like the one on page 73. And yet this same

Watch a colour scheme become more complex:

1 Start with a simple contrast, tawny orange against blue-green
2 Add cushions in terracotta: OK, but samey
3 Surprise colours – chalky-pink, aqua – give a needed lift
4 The last addition, magenta, oversteps the mark, deadening an appealing colour scheme. A mere fillip of magenta, however, might have been quite good (see *below*).

magenta, used in tiny doses such as a pattern on the yellow or pink, or even piping round some of the cushions, could have fizzed the whole ensemble up further still colour-wise without, so to speak, breaking the tension. This sort of playfulness with colour, pushing a harmony to the edge of breakdown, is something many painters pursue for precisely the excitement and tension it generates; and this development in (mainly) twentieth-century art is inevitably reflected in our interior decoration.

One last point: cushions can be over-played, but there is no cheaper way to try out ideas about colour in real rooms. Everyone needs cushions, and you can hardly have too many. Think of them as pawns in your colour chess-game.

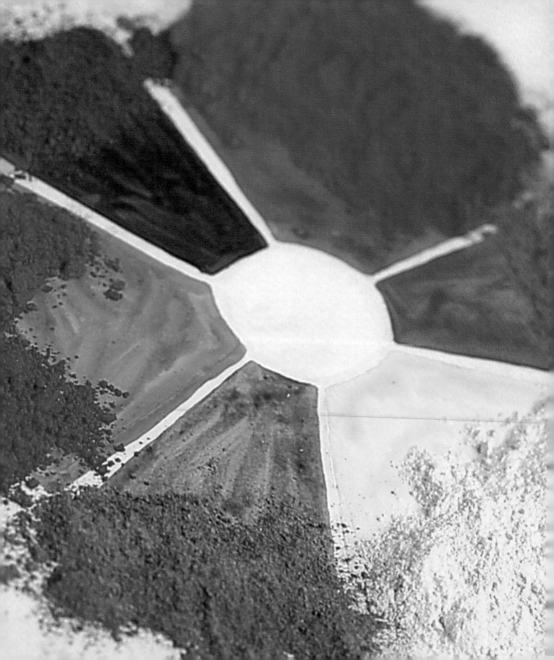

COLOUR THEORY

Entire books have been devoted to colour theory. They are mainly intended for fine artists, and are of little practical use to people who want to devise successful decorating colour schemes. I personally am not a great subscriber to colour theory as it is often peddled. But there is a lot to learn from fine artists, their intimate understanding of colour, and its behaviour, and anyone can do this just by looking. In fact, a detail from a painting by a great colourist like Bonnard or Matisse can tell you more about the power and magic of pure colour, the effect of a counterpoint of hues, than any colour theory device. Don't despise postcard reproductions: looked at on its own, a cropped-down section of one, with colours you respond to, can speak volumes.

But as you start out on your colour quest, slightly distrustful of your instincts (however right they may turn out to be) it can be comforting to have a slightly more universal system to hand. The colour wheel, the classic example of this, offers some basic guidelines to what to put with what, and why.

THE COLOUR WHEEL

As the picture opposite shows, a colour wheel is made up of six colours: the three 'primary' or primitive colours (red, blue and yellow) which cannot be mixed from any other combination of colours; and the three 'secondary' colours (orange, green and violet) made by intermixing two adjacent primaries. Thus **red + yellow = orange; red + blue = purple or violet; blue + yellow = green.**

Complementary colours are those which lie opposite each other on the colour wheel, whether primaries or secondaries. Thus red and green are complementary, as are yellow and purple, etc. In theory, complementaries 'go' well together and achieve a colour balance: a splash of red will give necessary and visually acceptable relief to a room which is predominantly green, and vice versa. In practice, because most room schemes involve many more colours and shades of colour, the solution cannot be so tidy, although some use of a complementary is invariably enlivening. But perhaps the most practical use of these colours is as a way to soften their opposite numbers without 'dirtying' them. A brash red paint, for instance, can be tamed by mixing in a little green; and so on, round the wheel. Adding some of a colour's complementary softens it without changing its hue — its redness, blueness etc. — its essence, as it were.

SHADES, TONES AND UNDERTONES

Isaac Newton discovered that white light — daylight — contains all the colours in the colour wheel and demonstrated this by angling light through a prism which separated it out into all the colours of the spectrum. Major scientific discovery though this was, it is of less practical concern to home decorators than the immense, extended family of shades, tones and, especially undertones, that are derived from the prismatic hues. Understanding, or recognizing, these can make a whole lot of difference when you are mixing or matching, or simply trying to put several colours together with success and *élan*.

Shades and tones Although these terms are often used almost interchangeably, they are in fact descriptions of different gradations of colour from a basic hue. If we take a vivid, clear green as a starting-point, innumerable shades can be arrived at by adding increasing amounts of white — moving towards whiteness in one direction

The blue-green at centre moves in four rapid stages towards white in one direction, and black in the other, by adding more white or black, respectively. On a commercial colour card this process will be considerably extended, but remember that all the shades still derive from one parent.

— or increasing amounts of black, moving towards blackness in the other. It is easiest to visualize this as a ladder (as represented on many paint chip cards) with the defining hue in the middle, paler shades above and darker ones below. A decorating scheme built up entirely from shades of the same hue, or colour, is monochrome. It can be visually pleasing and restful (see pages 48 and 56) although it will probably need a dash of a contrasting or complementary colour to spark it up.

Tones describe different gradations of a hue towards warmth or coolness. Take any colour on the wheel — blue, for example — and add a little of one neighbour (green) or a touch of the other (purple). Blue-green will exhibit a warmer tone, blue-purple a cooler one. Similarly, a greenish yellow will have a cooler tone than an orange-yellow.

Undertones If there were such a thing as a completely pure hue, undertones might not be a problem. In fact, all hues have a tendency to carry undertones and identifying them is critical to successful paint mixing, and also important in assembling room colours. Confusion arises because, at a cursory glance, especially under artificial light, the undertone of a colour may not declare itself. Blues which look relatively indistinguishable in the hand or on a paint chart may reveal very different, and possibly uncongenial, undertones expanded over the four walls of a room, in a carpet underfoot or over yards of fabric. A blue with a purple undertone is a different animal from a blue with a green one. To some eyes the difference is immediately apparent, to others not, and many uneasy colour schemes are the result of failing to spot and identify the undertone. Some people get away with combining warm greeny blue walls and a cool violet-blue carpet, but they are either professional decorators, breaking rules for a particular effect — or lucky. To find the undertone in a colour, try mixing a little white into it. The pastel that results will be more visibly cool or warm toned.

The importance of undertones is particularly relevant when you are trying to mix a paint colour. Suppose you want to 'tweak' a shelf red towards a soft raspberry. You must first decide whether raspberry is a cool or warm red, that is, whether it has a violet-blue or orange undertone. Violet-blue you decide, correctly.

Next, you need to identify a shelf colour in that tonal area, a blue-red rather than an orange-red like vermilion. It will probably be too dark, too strong, even too blue, going on crimson. Adding white very cautiously, a touch at a time, may correct this. But perhaps it is now *too* pink, a cold pink, moreover, that reveals a stronger blue undertone than you recognized at first glance. At this point I would tend to add a warm, brownish red like burnt sienna (cautiously again) rather than an orange-

Thinning out a paint to transparency, as shown with this range of colours, will deliver the undertone.

This is essential to know when you are mixing colours, or putting together a room scheme.

red, because the yellow-orange undertone of the latter combined with the bluish undertone of the original red will tend to merge into a greenish undertone. (Green is complementary to red so this *could* work, but only if the ratio is just right.) This is a hypothetical instance, described to give some idea of the relevance of undertones in paint mixing. If the process looks unduly taxing, believe me, it only takes a little experiment, a few (small, if you go slow) mistakes, and more *looking* for the whole business to become instinctive, or second nature.

Reading the projects, or colour exercises, in this book should fill in gaps and round out these suggestions. The

The same red, left, modified to create a more subtle shade using (from top) its complementary green, raw umber and purple-crimson.

The different results show the significance of undertones when working with colour.

nervous apprentice should start by adopting a safe approach like the colour schemes we begin with. Most people are cautious at first and choose white, cream, string, buff, grey, pale pastels. But a day may come when an invasion of vivid colour from a bunch of flowers, an ethnic rug, cushions or a dazzling new scarf suddenly supplies the missing colour you didn't even know you needed. One colour usually leads to another, so a decorative scheme that started out muted or negative works up to become positive and adventurous — and that is where the fun starts.

COLOUR AND TEXTURE

In my experience, home decorators frequently overlook the vital effect that texture — shiny, matt, shaggy, smooth — has on the look of a given colour and the way it performs in a room scheme. To take a simple example, a chenille and a furnishing cotton dyed with an identical shade will emerge looking considerably different. The chenille, being lustrous and richly textured, will have a greater depth and warmth of colour than the matt cotton. Similarly, a matt wall paint colour may appear to be a perfect match to a carpet swatch but the carpet, once laid, may look surprisingly different, due not simply to the depth of pile but also to the way natural light strikes a floor covering, as against a wall finish. The sensible way to cope with problems like these is to go with the colour you like in the more expensive material (chenille and carpet in the examples above) and work round this until you find the best combination of colour and texture.

Aiming for an exact match in different fabrics, trimmings, carpets and paints is always likely to be a headache. It is much better to settle for a related, lighter or deeper shade or a clean contrast. Judging from letters I get, most people come unstuck with trimmings — braid, fringes, bobbles, whatever. These may not seem important items but they can be costly when they are stretched over yards of curtaining, sofas, etc. and the wrong choice can unbalance a whole scheme. For starters, many trimmings are made from synthetic fibres to keep the cost down and tend to look different to natural fibres, once in place, and over a large area. As a natural-fibre fan, I used to buy yards of the cheapest cotton rug-fringe and dye it myself. If you decide to do this, a useful tip is to bundle the fringe into a pillowcase and dye it a lighter shade or colour than the one you originally think of. The

pillowcase helps to prevent it tangling up (especially if you dye in the washing machine) and a lighter shade usually looks better over a large area. I dyed yards of fringe deep green to border bed-hangings made from a vibrant 1930s rose-printed fabric, a linen union in which dark green was the strongest colour, and have been kicking myself ever since for not matching the fringe colour to the neutral, tawny background shade of the fabric. In the hand the dark leaf green looked striking. On the finished bed, it is both too much and too dark. Such misjudgements are easily made, but usually repented too late when the trimming is in place and sadly fails to match up with your 'vision'.

Everyone makes mistakes of this sort. Ask any decorator. The positive side is that they teach you more than easy successses do. Again, ask any decorator, or at least ask a friendly, helpful one — sadly, some will maintain they never put a foot wrong from the outset.

TEXTURE VIA PAINT

The near-impossibility of thinking of colour apart from texture is particularly clear with paints, where an identical colour-mix in two different textures — shiny and matt to take an obvious example — look noticeably dissimilar because of the way the shiny surface reflects the light. I discovered this for myself when I bought the same colour, a very dark green, in two different formulations: a matt emulsion for walls, and an eggshell finish for woodwork. They looked identical in their cans, but quite different when they were brushed out on their respective surfaces. The eggshell looked many shades lighter and I had to add a fair bit of tinting colour — black and a little ultramarine — to arrive at a uniform shade around the room. This is something to watch out for when you are trying to match up matt and low-sheen

Tinting agents can behave differently in diferent paint media. Here, the same amount of raw sienna was mixed into the quantity of each range of base paints. The resultant colour is as different as palest cream to warm tan.

Clear varnish

Soft distemper

Acrylic scumble

Limewash

Oil scumble

Impasto

Emulsion

Pure linseed oil

25

or shiny paints from a commercial range, whatever the colour in question. The fact that one paint was a water-based acrylic emulsion, and the other an oil-based alkyd, only emphasized the difference.

The simplest way to gain an understanding of this colour/texture symbiosis is by considering how a certain colour behaves when it is mixed with very different textures of paint. This is the route most home decorators opt for as it is both familiar and relatively inexpensive.

The swatches shown on page 25 demonstrate how one pigment, a raw sienna powder colour, shows up when it is mixed with a variety of mediums or binders. These range from pasty distemper to highly transparent linseed oil and include varnish, emulsion paint, scumble glaze and limewash. In each case the same quantity of pigment was dissolved in the appropriate solvent for the medium — water for water-based paints, white spirit for oil-based ones, methylated spirits for shellac — and mixed into the 'base'. As our samples show, the characteristics of each medium made the raw sienna colour look subtly or widely different. The oily, transparent bases clearly deliver a greatly increased intensity of colour and most of the finishes look similar in tone. The water-based paints — limewash, soft distemper and a vinyl silk emulsion — which contain a high proportion of extenders and pasty substances like chalk or polymers, remain ghostly by comparison. What is more, these water-based paints look different from each other because of their different basic ingredients and the extent to which these 'overwhelm' the tinting agent. It is a fact that much less pigment is needed to colour limewash than soft distemper. Since pigment is the costliest ingredient in both paints, distemper tended to be used in pastel shades as an interior finish only, whereas limewash was — and still is — made up in richer colours from tawny yellow to deep terracotta for both interior and exterior use.

It would have been quite possible to 'tint up' the paler swatches to match the rest, simply by using more pigment, but we felt this would have diluted the message: that texture alters colour dramatically. This can be translated into fabrics, to some extent. A fine-textured, absorbent fabric with a sheen — pure silk is an example — has pretty much the same visual effect as our transparent-medium (varnish, scumble glaze or linseed oil) swatches, whereas close-woven, dense fabrics, like canvas, cotton or linen, resemble the paler swatches. The nature of materials, and their effect upon colour, is often overlooked in a frustrating search for the perfect 'match' between, say, a cotton print and a synthetic fibre trim.

It is worth registering how various mediums affect the same colour, or a similar one, as this will have a bearing on your overall room scheme. The colour in old-fashioned 'chalky', matt, textured paints like limewash and distemper looks 'soft'. The same one in a plastic-based paint like emulsion is more even and opaque, but somewhat 'hard' and 'dead', and needs enlivening with pictures and objects to soften and break up this uniformity of tone and texture. Transparent finishes like oil- or acrylic-based glazes are splendidly flattering to problem spaces, softening, disguising and generally 'blurring' the architectural data, but they need firmness in the detail of an interior (picture frames, rugs, a touch of black) if they are not to look too wishy-washy for contemporary taste.

Appreciating these different effects will add to your understanding of colour and so lead to greater confidence and control, not just in handling paints — which is only one form of colour in decoration — but across the whole range of materials that make up a room scheme: fabrics, carpet, rugs, painted furniture, etc. Light, too, can affect colour dramatically. To take one example, a roller blind with daylight shining through it looks completely different to the same blind lit by electric light.

A shell-pink by night may look alarmingly vivid, hot pink going on coral, with sunshine coming through. The opposite is true of lampshades, whose colouring springs to life at night.

Textured paints and finishes Perhaps as a reaction to the flat 'plastic' look of so much emulsion wall paint, there is a growing interest in walls with textured finishes, which may or may not be coloured. They add warmth and interest to a room, especially one with a low-key colour scheme. I am not talking about the crude, exaggerated textures created by stippling or combing a proprietary finishing compound to create giant goose-pimples, whorls or fan patterns. Textured finishes have come a long way recently and are available in a wide range of products, from traditional to high-tech, with effects that go from subtle to dramatic.

Limewash Made from lime putty copiously thinned with water, this is one of the earliest and simplest paints. Tint with earth pigments in powder form for traditional Tuscan colours. As our samples show, limewash colours have a glow and intensity all their own. The paint, applied as thin as milk, dries opaque with a gritty, chalky texture that looks soft but actually is as hard as the limestone it is made from. The ideal coating for lime plaster or render, it is also effective on porous surfaces like brick, breeze blocks, aged cement render and

Traditional limewash will give gloriously pure, vivid colours when mixed with dry pigments; this is due partly to the refractiveness of the lime.

new gypsum plaster. Surfaces should be sprayed with water until they are damp before application. A base coat of untinted — white — limewash helps to build colour, but as many as five coats may be needed for colours like the ones shown here. Conservationists prefer limewash on old buildings because it allows the fabric to 'breathe'.

Soft distemper Made of chalk soaked in water then bound with animal glue and tinted with dry pigments, this is one of the prettiest traditional interior finishes with a matt, powdery texture. It can be used on most surfaces, but is thick and slow to apply, and is not washable. In the right place — a bedroom, say — it can last for decades with occasional re-touching.

Whitewash In this context I don't mean the traditional, all-over-white farmyard kind of paint, but a hi-tech product with historic roots that is available in the United States, and whose effect is to give walls the finest ridgy surface like microscopic pin-tucks. Its modern version, Old Village Whitewash, was developed by the historic preservation team working at Colonial Williamsburg, Virginia. It can be over-painted with emulsion or left its own pleasant calico white.

The brown, red and yellow here are mixed with earth pigments; the blues with pure ultramarine, and ultramarine with yellow added.

Impasto Impasto is not dissimilar to whitewash but has a softer look and heavier consistency, somewhere between paint and plaster. It is useful on poor walls, where it works as a filler as well as paint and can be brushed out for a soft distemper look or roughed up for an 'old walls' effect. A light colourwash gives unemphatic colour which picks up on the irregularities attractively. It can be over-painted, or you can tint it in the can although this may look 'heavy' by comparison. It makes a splendid ceiling paint, a matt, warm-toned white.

Marmorino A new product developed by Paint Magic, this imitates ancient stucco finishes (see opposite). It is a versatile material, applied with a plasterer's steel float, which bonds with virtually any substrate and can give remarkable textural contrast with two layers only 1mm thick. It can deliver the 'old plaster' look shown here or, more evenly spread and worked over, a polished stucco sheen. The Marmorino can be tinted integrally with dissolved pigment, or colourwashed when dry for a softer effect which emphasizes texture. It can be waxed for a higher shine but I prefer it matt, as here. A tough water- and damp-resistant finish for both interior and exterior use, it is expensive compared with paint but cheap compared with laborious, complex, hand-crafted versions. Designers, decorators love it.

COLOUR ON WOOD

Transparent colour as a wood finish has come to the fore in recent years in the wake of its use on walls, and is proving popular both as a fast way to even up floorboards, usually with a 'driftwood' effect in mind, and as a test run on wooden furniture whose owners feel the need for a splash of colour but are not confident enough to leap into a solid paint finish. Which is not to say that transparent colour on wood is not attractive in itself. It is, as our accompanying patchwork of samples demonstrates. Indeed, most customers who try these effects out experimentally remain with them — their charm is that they colour without masking the grain and texture of the wood itself. This adds character and warmth, while the transparency of the finish means that a large piece will not loom too large, and 'settles' easily into its environment. Last, and by no means least, these water-based washes, or stains, are delightfully quick to apply with a brush, rags or pads, whichever is handiest. I always keep rags close by in any case, to smooth out or lighten the colour as necessary. One or two coats of a clear matt varnish will protect the surface, although floors may need touching up from time to time.

The one snag with these woodwashes is that the wood must be clean and bare to start with, to allow the water-based colour to penetrate and stain the surface. Floors finished with varnish or sealant can be sanded clean with a hired, industrial-type sander. Waxed wood is cleaned with white spirit and pads of soft wire wood. The tricky one is new, factory-finished 'pine', more often knotty deal, which has been sprayed with a melamine-type plastic coating that is tough and almost impossible to remove. Our recommendation in such cases is to forget transparent colour or trying to strip off the factory finish, and to coat the piece (well cleaned, of course) with a product like sand 'n' seal shellac or acrylic convertor which, when

dry, allows water-based paints to bond with the plastic coating. If a client still wants a non-solid finish, our usual advice is to try distressing in two colours, as shown on some of our picture frames in the room sets, which gives a broken colour effect, or dry-brushing. When the woodwash is dry, varnish with a matt acrylic varnish to seal the surface but keep the feel of natural wood.

ONE COLOUR, THREE VERSIONS

OPAQUE TO TRANSPARENT COLOUR

People today are more familiar with transparent paint effects — glazes or washes — than they were fifteen years ago when I wrote *Paint Magic*. But some uncertainty remains about what they 'do' for an interior, and how they compare with the same colour applied opaquely. Our mini room-set was small enough to test out three versions of the same colour — a tawny orange emulsion paint called 'Flowerpot' — applied opaque from the tin, mixed into a clear colourwash base for a transparent wash, and 'knocked back', for interest, with a watery white wash. In each case, the chair, frame and skirting were finished with a blue-green called 'Sea Blue', more to underline the story than because they necessarily look better that way. I think the different results are instructive, and may help you see how a given space is changed by modifying the various paints used.

SOLID, OPAQUE COLOUR This is the boldest way to use strong colour and when the colours are complementary, as here, the effect is positive without being a smack in the eye. In fact, the overall look is calm rather than otherwise, enhanced by the matt texture throughout and the cooling and reflective whitewashed floorboards. Strong colours make spaces look smaller, and somewhat darker, which can be a disadvantage. On the other hand, a strong or dark colour used uninterruptedly in a room — on woodwork, cupboards and shelving as well as walls — can make it seem larger by unifying all its elements, rather in the way that dressing in one unbroken colour tends to make people look taller and slimmer. Strong colour on walls tends to call for equally dense and weighty shades elsewhere — a pale pink chair here, for instance, would have been overwhelmed. This is not to suggest that you paint everything in a room in different, intense shades. Unless you are assured in your use of colour, go about it bit by bit, leaving time in between for your eye to appraise the new relationship. Always try out new colour ingredients experimentally, using fabrics, plates or whatever props come to hand, to determine what is missing. It may be a strong contrast — black, crimson, deep blue — or a spark of a 'rogue' colour, in small doses, that wakes up the overall scheme. Here, for instance, it might be a hot pink, lime green or dark-brown-red.

TRANSPARENT COLOURWASH This effect, of a pale base showing up through a blurry, matt transparent colour, has been likened to fresco, old Tuscan walls and watercolour painting — where the word 'wash' stems from. Over the past few years, colourwash has taken over to some extent from oil glaze finishes because its freshness and informality, a sort of painterly looseness, suit contemporary tastes better. However, people who like their transparent finishes smooth and have perfect walls will be more comfortable with a finely stippled, tinted oil glaze. Be warned, though, that oil glazes invariably yellow over time — avoid pale blue unless you don't mind it turning to aqua. Acrylic-based transparent glaze, sold as acrylic scumble, is non-yellowing but sets more rapidly than oil-based so perfect smoothness is harder to achieve.

Our colourwash was made by mixing the 'Flowerpot' emulsion into clear colourwash to maintain colour consistency. We applied the wash over an off-white vinyl silk emulsion, using a decorator's sponge to 'wipe' the colour rapidly over the base, and a softening brush to smooth out and even up the wet surface. The chair was finished with a blue-green tinted acrylic scumble over an off-white base, and the skirting and frame were dry-brushed and distressed in the same colours to arrive at what painters call 'broken colour'.

In our mini room-set the striking characteristic of transparent wall finishes is clearly visible: a warm, back-lit glow, the result of the light being reflected back from the pale base. This holds true whether the wash/glaze is warm- or cool-toned. Transparent colour has a special radiance that opaque colour cannot deliver. Our colour-washed set looks sunny compared to the solid-coloured

one, although both were photographed in identical natural lighting, on a cloudy day. Even if this noticeable warmth and radiance is an optical illusion, it has endeared these finishes to people who live in grey climates, or who are trying to warm up dark, bleak or north-facing rooms. Warm tones, pink, yellow, tawny orange and terracotta always introduce a sunny quality. Conversely, in hot climates, cool blues and greens in transparent finishes have a watery quality, like sunlight on the sea, which is refreshing and pretty.

Another optical trick that these finishes deliver is an apparent increase in size. Spaces look larger, 'opened out' in a surprising way. This is only hinted at in our tiny set; the full impact can only really be appreciated on a full room scale. If your problem is confined space — a narrow hall, poky little rooms with low ceilings — transparent colour is a valuable tool. Its softening effect is also helpful in playing down skimpy, fast-fix joinery — mean skirting, flat doors, built-in cupboards. Painting a run of cupboards to match the walls is a sure-fire way to pull a small room together and give it a classier, finished look. Be sure to apply a protective coat of varnish, preferably a clear, matt, non-yellowing acrylic on any woodwork. These transparent finishes are not tough and require sealing in heavy-duty situations.

WHITING OUT Our third example (opposite) shows how dramatically a transparent white wash can soften and neutralize a vivid wall colour, giving a chalky bloom which is cool and subtle. We applied the 'whitewash' (clear colourwash tinted with white pigment) directly over the opaque version of 'Flowerpot'. This is clearly an idea which could be useful for toning down a wall colour that turns out to be several tones brighter on the wall than it is in the can or on the swatch. This is the remedial aspect of whiting out. Considerably faster than completely painting over the

garish colour, it can come up with a mysteriously attractive result. It can also be used deliberately, as in one designer friend's interior where a mural based on classical motifs was first painted in fiercely vivid colours — orange, scarlet, purple, emerald — then whited over entirely so that these colours 'ghosted' through, distinct but misted over. The effect was sophisticated, with something of the look of faded frescos, and very attractive, but it would need confidence in the end result to achieve it successfully.

To round things off we softened the other elements to match by the simple device of dry-brushing with white over the solid blue-greens. This is a quick, fun way to 'knock back' over-bright colours that have got out of hand in a room scheme and is especially successful on painted furniture and woodwork. The name — dry-brushing — says it all. A brush is dipped into white paint, then brushed out on paper until it noticeably 'drags' leaving sparse thin marks. At this point it is brushed lightly but firmly over the painted surface until the solid colour is broken up and retreats visually. Dry-brushing can be done smoothly, or sketchily, to give a more rustic look. It will need varnishing, but stick to a matt varnish. The technique is not, of course, restricted to the remedial; decorative painters often dry-brush positive colour over a white, or light, base for a streaky, rustic finish that goes very well with the homely lines of country furniture, both old and reproduction. It is a pretty, fast way to bring out detail and add interest to painted surfaces, but it needs to be done with a sparing touch. Always stand back frequently to gauge the effect, otherwise it will end up just as 'rustic dragging', pleasant but not quite the same thing.

A COLOUR-GO-ROUND

RESCUING COLOUR When paint colours go wrong, a transparent glaze may save the day more rapidly and inexpensively than re-painting. All four swatches in our little demonstration (overleaf) of how dramatically and variously transparent glazes can soften, age or transform a given 'bright' shade began with the sharp lime green emulsion paint used on the central tablet. Of course, the same game can be played with muted base colours but the aim here was to show the maximum alteration possible.

Reading clockwise, the first glaze colour (using dry pigment dissolved in water and mixed into acrylic scumble glaze) is plain white, an idea also shown on a larger scale on page 48. As you can see, it 'knocks back' the base shade effectively, a handy trick for softening and cooling down wall colours or furniture paints that have gone over the top. You need to work fast glazing walls, preferably with someone to help you, to even out the scumble before it 'sets off' or hardens unmanageably — the 'open time' is 8–12 minutes depending on conditions in the room.

The second glaze is made up with the complementary (see page 17) to yellow-green — a mauve-pink. This largely 'neutralizes' the lime green sharpness and acid-ity and creates one of those mysterious no-colour colours, ambiguous but attractive, which can look splendid in the right context. Layering subtly different-coloured glazes gives indefinable colours of great depth which make a flattering background, a sort of 'super-neutral'.

For the third sample, which shows a light 'antiquing' treatment, we used a little burnt umber to shade and 'dirty' the lime green base. Raw umber would have pro-duced a greener ageing. This is a standard finishing device on painted furniture, to mimic time-softened colours. It is infallibly effective but needs sensitive handling, on walls especially, not to look merely grubby.

Lastly, another green glaze, but a blue rather than yellow-green one, creates a whole new shade of green, predominantly cool toned but underlit, as it were, by its acid base. This too is a regularly used device, usually achieved by working within contrasting tones of one colour to create something of a 'shot silk' ambiguity of tone, softer and richer than any effect delivered by either colour used alone. This is the perennial fascination, and challenge, of glaze work or transparent colour.

WHITE ON WHITE No one feels threatened by white as a decorating colour because, in theory at least, it goes with everything: old, new, bright, faded. White walls, woodwork, cornices, ceilings create a pristine space, light-filled and undemanding in terms of colour skills. You can hardly go wrong with white. As is well known, artists prefer it as a background to paintings and sculpture. Architects love white because it focuses attention on space and form, the bone structure of building. When people consult me about colour schemes for a newly acquired property — house, cottage or apartment — I often suggest 'whiting out' as a wise first move. It is practical in the sense that it provides an excellent base for further decoration, but also helpful aesthetically because it lets you see exactly what you have got to work with, without distractions.

All the same, in my view there is a downside to white as a predominant decorating colour. In a northern climate, with grey skies much of the year, it can look bleak, comfortless, even clinical, and it is only human to crave the warmth and visual nourishment of colour. This may not be a problem for painters who can people their snowy interiors with canvases, but a few prints, which may be all that new home-owners have collected, cannot make such a brave statement.

White is also demanding technically and practically. For starters, it needs to be what decorators call 'a good white'. The 'brilliant whites' which dominate standard paint ranges all have a blue undertone. This may look sparkling on window-frames in a brick wall, but as an overall interior decorating colour it creates a chilly environment, akin to the 'snow light' of Scandinavian interiors in winter. White for our purposes (forget optics) embraces a myriad subtly different tones: creamy, silvery, greyed, pinkish. Magnolia, the universally preferred 'off-white' for decades, has a faintly creamy pink cast designed to take the chill off visually.

Whichever white tone you choose, it needs to be applied solidly, opaquely, so that no tinge of 'shadow' — due to dark base colours — surfaces in patches. This can call for many coats of paint — five to seven, according to a painter of the old perfectionist school I once talked to. The dazzling white, limewashed walls of the Greek islands, once seen never forgotten, owe their brilliance to the sheer depth of their layers which are refurbished yearly, a procedure made possible by the watery thinness of limewash. Many thin coats is still the skilled tradesman's rule for success — which eliminates most one-coat, thixotropic convenience paints.

White woodwork *en suite* with walls is also problematic because it requires extra care in preparation, 'prepping' in painter parlance: thorough sanding and filling, and many applications of paint, progressing from primer to finishing coat, with careful smoothing in between to remove grit, hairs, dust, etc. White focuses attention on imperfections over time because they inevitably collect grime and dust; and washing down periodically only emphasizes this. Maintenance, in short, is probably the main disadvantage of an 'all-white' interior scheme; great when spanking new, it is insidiously depressing when it begins to look grubby, discoloured, neglected.

Having stressed the demanding aspects of white in decoration, I should add in fairness that when it is well executed nothing looks more beautiful, airy and serene in the right — hot, sunny — climate. In these conditions a simple whitewash is mysteriously restful. For northerly situations the option, described below, is to work out the white ploy through a range of contrasting textures — shiny, frosty, furry, silky, chalky — relying on natural materials as well as subtly varied tones and textures of paint. The fun comes in inventing or experimenting with your own variant: white pebbles instead of marble mantelpieces, painted wicker rather than painted wood, towelling instead of wool, muslin instead of silk.

White on white is a formula made chic by legendary interior decorator, Syrie Maugham, whose glamorous London drawing room dispelled any notion that all-white need look bleak or austere. Recognizing that white is subtly altered by a change of texture, she brought together chalky matt or shiny lacquer surfaces, fur and wool rugs, satin cushions and linen covers, white marble and whitewashed wood. Reflected back by tall mirrored screens, the effect was dazzling, a radically new interpretation of metropolitan elegance which was much admired and copied.

Syrie Maugham's development of the white-on-white theme was anything but practical, its costly upkeep making it all the more alluring. But her basic idea, of playing off as many different white textures as possible, is one that still holds good — and is easily reproduced on a limited scale and a small budget.

It starts with natural materials. As our theme picture shows, nature is full of pleasing variations on the white theme: shells, pebbles, flowers, bleached driftwood, marble, bones. White fabrics can be as various as muslin, cotton, linen, wool and raw silk — all washable. White paint can be slick and shiny, opalescent like mother-of-pearl, or matt like sugar icing. Or it can be thinned to a ghostly pallor, allowing the texture beneath — board floors, wicker — to contribute its own play of light and shade. We had some fun with contrasting textures in our white-on-white room set. Given the few elements involved, I think it suggests the amount of variety and texture that can be introduced with the simplest means. Aside from a fall of white muslin, it was all done with paint, exploiting the textural contrasts of different finishes and effects.

For the walls, we played around with the notion of glossy pattern applied with a stamp or stencil over a matt base (which gives the effect of cotton damask) but opted finally for a less subtle, but more noticeable, contrast between stripes of a pearly glaze alternating with a vinyl silk emulsion. A completely matt base might have yielded greater contrast but we feared an absorbent matt emulsion might have swallowed up the pearly glaze. Silk finish is less absorbent and is often recommended as a base for glazes. The result was effective and subtle, the pearly stripes mysteriously reflective and warmer in tone, like satin against the silky white base.

The floor of rough new planks was easily brought into the white-on-white story with a wash of thinned white acrylic emulsion. This was brushed on and wiped back with rags, to allow the texture to show through while disguising the knots and adding a suitably bleached effect. Pale floors dramatically enlarge the apparent size of a room as well as reflecting back any available natural light. A wash of white is a fast, effective treatment for knotty softwood planks, tempering their yellow colour and softening grain and knots to an overall pallor. At least two coats of a non-yellowing matt acrylic varnish should be applied on top of the treated boards to protect the surface and make cleaning easier.

For fun and variety, we gave the skirting a 'crackle glazed' finish. This was done in a just-off-white acrylic gloss over a putty-coloured base and was noticeable enough to show up in the final shot without detracting from the 'white' theme. Crackle glaze is a popular addition to the decorative painter's kit. It consists of a gloopy, slightly sticky substance, which is water-activated so that when it is brushed between two layers of standard emulsion paints the second coat rapidly breaks up

Contrast-striped walls: use a white vinyl silk or satin emulsion; mask off broad stripes at regular intervals and use a pearly glaze on alternate stripes for shimmering depth and warmth.

Bleach-effect floor: brush thinned acrylic gloss paint on to prepared bare boards; wipe back with rags while still wet to highlight the grain. Seal with at least two coats of non-yellowing acrylic varnish.

Crackleglazed skirting boards: over a puttyish emulsion base for accent and texture, apply first glaze, then an off-white gloss acrylic; allow to crackle, and seal immediately with shellac, then matt varnish when fully dry.

into a distinctive 'alligatored' surface. Seal immediately with a non-water-based spirit varnish like white polish; if protecting further, use a matt acrylic varnish.

The chair was painted with a straightforward white gloss, slightly tinted with ochre yellow for an ivory tinge. Gloss white is the poor man's white lacquer, with a high-shine slick finish that stands out against the subtle finishes used here. It is worth considering for its visual impact in any all-white setting. But be warned: gloss paint shows up every imperfection, gritty surfaces, cracks, clumsy filling jobs. Spend time on 'prepping', smoothing and rubbing down, for an impressive finish.

This left the picture frame. A roughed-up finish seemed called for here, to echo the rough floor and contrast with the walls. The current favourite look in this style is distressing — paint scraped or wire-wooled back to reveal an undercoat colour while at the same time hinting at the erosion of time and use. A distressed finish takes away from the 'factory new' blandness of a perfect paint job. Judiciously introduced, it is a simple way to add a touch of ruggedness and charac-

'Lacquer' chair: simply painted with white gloss tinted to ivory with ochre yellow to stand out against the matt white surfaces.

'Silver leaf' distressed picture frame: use metallic silver paint as a base, then when dry roughly rub over with a candle. Apply standard white emulsion, and rub back with steel wool when dry.

ter. To keep within our shades of white theme, the distressing was done with standard white emulsion over a base of silver paint. Metallic paints look crude on their own, but shining here and there through a distressed paint surface their glitter enlivens the result impressively — and just as effectively as a more expensive and time-consuming coat of silver or aluminium leaf.

The 'finishing touch', as the glossies put it, would be a fall of white muslin, introducing just enough softness and translucency to our microcosmic white-on-white set to remind anyone interested in this theme of the important part fabrics play in the final result. Calico, lace, cotton duck, or silk, satin and velveteen, could all contribute their own sensuous quality — crisp, rugged, frail, seductively reflective or warmly inviting — to a similar scenario. Add the sparkle of mirrors, the frostiness of etched glass, the opalescence of mother-of-pearl, the 'thinginess' of white pebbles, and it becomes clear that this apparently drastically limited decorating palette is rich in subtle visual possibilities.

LOW-KEY NEUTRALS Essentially these are *the* background colours, in decoration as in nature: laid back, relaxing, restful. As our theme picture shows, they can range through straw pale to nut brown, taking in many subtle shades along the way, but most echo the natural tones of stone, wood, sand, dry foliage. However, there are many families of neutrals, taking the word loosely, and we show a newly fashionable one in our second mini-room. Perhaps what they all share is a monochromatic — one colour — tendency, even though they move through many tones, shades and textures. They can be austerely sophisticated, as in much recent architecture, or as homely as a log-cabin. Having said that, I see neutrals in decoration as a metropolitan theme, creating a peaceful oasis, a retreat from the rush and hassle of daily life. Men unquestionably favour them, and designers enjoy playing the neutral game because it takes skill — and quality 'stuff' — to prevent them looking bland and impersonal. Think of all those hotel lobbies and big business foyers. The risk with neutrals is they can look safe — even boring.

As with the white-on-white ploy, the secret of handling neutrals well is to play the textures for all you are worth. There is no shortage of these. All the straws and wickers and unbleached natural fibres, coir, hessian and linen, contrast with the warm sheen of polished wood, the biscuit texture of travertine, rough stone or sand-blasted concrete. Then, stepping up the colour intensity a little, there are richly mottled surfaces like tortoiseshell or vinegar graining, dark marble, unglazed pottery, ivory or bone, tribal rugs. Add a modicum of black, for backbone, metallic surfaces — gilt, chrome, pewter — for lustre, and some spots of pure colour, and you have a refined, subtle interior that any tycoon, male or female, would slip into as comfortably as a pair of loafers, while recognizing that the ambience can also

strike the right polished note for other business types and for corporate entertaining.

The safari room set 'Safari' is a name plucked out of the air, but it seems to fit the simple going-on-sophisticated neutrals shown here: a putty wall colour (pale khaki) contrasted with ivory gloss, bone white, warm vinegar graining in tortoiseshell mode, and a happenstance prop, an ethnic sun helmet in greenish straw with leather trimmings.

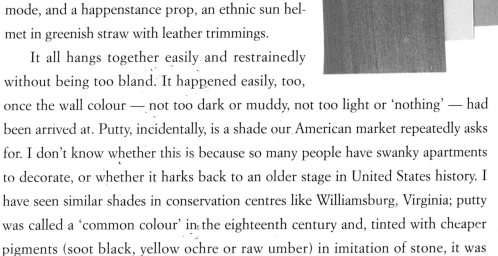

It all hangs together easily and restrainedly without being too bland. It happened easily, too, once the wall colour — not too dark or muddy, not too light or 'nothing' — had been arrived at. Putty, incidentally, is a shade our American market repeatedly asks for. I don't know whether this is because so many people have swanky apartments to decorate, or whether it harks back to an older stage in United States history. I have seen similar shades in conservation centres like Williamsburg, Virginia; putty was called a 'common colour' in the eighteenth century and, tinted with cheaper pigments (soot black, yellow ochre or raw umber) in imitation of stone, it was deemed highly suitable for halls and staircases.

We tinted up a stone-coloured emulsion paint with raw umber and a touch of black for the putty wall shade. The skirting was painted a matt ivory white to contrast with the walls and the warmly stained and polished boards. Some gloss seemed called for and we used a warmer, cream-to-bone shade on the chair. It all looked handsome, but a touch austere, so the vinegar-grained picture frame fell into

Putty/khaki walls: try tinting up a standard emulsion to create your own shade using universal stainers, in raw umber, black and yellow ochre.

Stained floorboards: use a warm shade and stain and seal well; use 2 coats gloss varnish for deep shine.

SAFARI

Ivory skirting board: provides contrast with the putty walls and rich floor; use a matt ivory white wood paint to foil the floor's sheen.

place with its russet-brown-black colouring and old sepia-toned portrait! The splendid sun-helmet, a gift from a travelling sister, happily combined putty to russet shades in one package and tied the scheme up neatly.

In one sense you can't go far wrong with this decorating palette because, as we found, the colours, or shades, are highly compatible and settle down together like big cats in the African veld. On a large scale — throughout an apartment — they

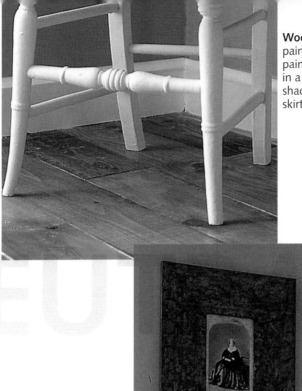

Wooden chair: painted with gloss paint to stand out, in a warmer cream shade than the skirting.

Vinegar-grained picture frame: warms up and accents the quiet neutrals, especially with a sepia-tinted picture. Any artwork will stand out very well against this background wall colour.

could look a little drab, or a touch melancholy, in glum weather. However, there is no need for this. A neutral background is the ideal backdrop for paintings, including the wildest, and for artworks of all kinds — not to mention found objects like driftwood, shells, pebbles, rusty metal … The charm of neutrals is that just one bunch of flowers, one rug or one pink or red cushion, has such impact that you seem to be relishing pure colour properly for the first time.

NEUTRALS II This colour scheme turned up in one of my shop windows while I was thinking about neutrals and it looked so cool and clean that I hi-jacked the pieces and set them up in our mini room-set. I think the colours might fairly be described as neutral in my interpretation of these, as tending towards monochrome. Here the basic ones are blue, off-white and silver, a combination that suggests snowy landscapes or the chorus in Swan Lake. The set shows a prettier and more feminine use of a neutral colour scheme, with the darker grey-blue lamp and chair as defining shapes against a cool but glamorous silver and white background. Note that none of the white shades are 'brilliant white' which, with its blue undertone, would look too chilly.

The star here is undoubtedly the folding screen with its simple but highly effective blocks of silvery (actually aluminium) leaf alternating with off-white. The idea owes something to traditional Japanese screens where decorative use is made of slightly overlapping squares of gold leaf.

The neutral feeling of this little set would be lost, incidentally, if the blue was a vivid shade like the one featured on page 73, or if it had a greeny undertone. Here it is blue-grey, and grey and silver have an obvious affinity. It is interesting that whereas blue-and-white in the manner of blue and white china or a *Toile de Jouy* print looks crisp and lively, the mood set by these greyed tones is meditative and gentle. Just another example of the mysterious potency of small colour changes.

SAFE AND SOFT: DRIED FLOWER SHADES Basically 'greyed' flower tones, from delicate pastels to near-jewel colours (crimson, purple, sapphire), these shades are perhaps the easiest to live with of all the palettes in this book — warm, but unemphatic, definitely 'there' in a restrained, background fashion. I see their provenance as 'English country house' because what 'lifts' them visually is the generous presence of chintz. From the nineteenth century onwards this historic, Indian glazed-cotton fabric, usually lavishly floral as to motif, linked aristocratic drawing rooms intimately and appropriately with the flower gardens beyond. Chintz was used for loose covers, invariably, as it was able to withstand wear and washing (though it lost its high sheen along the way), and was reasonably proof against dogs and chaps relaxing after a shoot or a hunt, and pretty enough to suggest a certain female claim on living rooms (as distinct from smoking rooms, billiard rooms, etc.) without being 'boudoir-ish'.

The 1980s and 1990s twist on these delectably gentle flower shades is Italianate. Wall, or enveloping, colours become warmer and textured, moving towards rich yellows, soft reds and terracotta instead of the cool pastel shades once favoured as a foil to patterned chintz. So for walls and painted furniture we see apricots, rosy red, blue-green, ochre yellows, the shades of old Tuscan walls, faded fabrics, worn gilding, old porcelain. 'Old', 'faded', 'worn' is perhaps the key to understanding this colour palette. I have seen it beautifully interpreted, *mutatis mutandis*, in tiny, eccentrically beamed cottages with a spatter of window types: Gothick, Regency. Perhaps the point to pick up on is that the rooms are outward looking, framing a cherished, husbanded view. When what you look out on is the main feature of an interior you need to go gently with colour.

Other colour references for these combinations might include Aubusson carpets, natural dyes used in heather-mixture tweeds, weathered bricks, sea-urchin shells, corals and semi-precious stones like amethyst, cornelian, amber, aquamarine. The palette is by no means restricted to pastels and the darker range would include peaty browns, seaweed greens, mellow yellows and sloe blue — but nothing sharp, hot or bright because these upset the balance. Black should be in there, though, in small, corrective doses — on picture

frames, japanned furniture or lamp bases — to stop it all getting too soft and pretty-pretty.

There is no simple rule-of-thumb for putting together a room scheme based on these muted colours. Getting it right is a matter of experiment, adding, subtracting and moving things around until instinct tells you that you are on the right track. I buy a lot of old textiles, often scraps, as colour references. Wrapping cushions in these is helpful when you are undecided. The successful rooms are invariably complex; their 'schemes' are not readable at a glance although everything hangs together undemandingly. They have 'atmosphere', something romantic and subtle which stays in the mind.

Our room-set version of these colours took longer than any of the others to 'click' (it was the length of old chintz that did the trick). I put this down to our deliberate policy of sticking with five basic elements every time — which goes against the grain with a look so bound up with bits and pieces, family possessions, old rugs, softened colours, cushions and flowers.

We learnt some useful lessons along the way. Transparent wall colours are help-

Colourwashed walls: this 'transparent' greyish pink gives the subtlety and painterly warmth of an Italian fresco; water down an emulsion and apply with a sponge, softening with a broad, dry brush, or buy a proprietary colourwash and tint to your desired shade.

Skirting board: like the floor, the base colour needed softening. We dry-brushed a grey/blue green matt paint with off-white.

ful in creating this floaty, poetic ambience and we used a greyish pink colourwash for its evocation of Italian frescos. In the 1980s this would have been an oil glaze finish, stippled or dragged, but in the 1990s the chalky clarity of a wash feels 'right' for the times — painterly, un-posh. All the other colours, the blue-green-grey for the chair and skirting, the matt grey-white of the washed floorboards, needed to be similarly 'softened' to work in our miniature set. We dry-brushed the solid paint colours with 'dirty white' to achieve this. We used only matt finishes, with no glitz or gleam although something of these would fit into a real room. We tried a raft of picture frames, and a silhouette picture (touch of black) and finally settled for the bunch of dried lavender. But it was the chintz fabric (shades of country house 'stuff') that pulled it together, talking up the existing colours and adding a splash of old-white for contrast, but without introducing discordant elements. The grey-pink

Dry-brushed chair: to match the skirting board, the same solid base was 'softened' with dry brushing. Remember that if you use emulsion on wood, you must seal well afterwards – and with a matt varnish to maintain the 'soft' mood.

Dried flower picture: a bunch of dried lavender provides a very 'country' motif, and the quintessential colour from this palette.

Fabrics: this chintz pulled everything together, combining both the existing colours and off-white, and could frame a window or define an upholstered chair; the warm tones of the rug provide a foundation for the room's visual effect.

to mulberry shades of an old rug (a car-boot-sale buy) on the boards also provided visual 'anchorage'. In other words, these soft, washy, ineffable colour schemes need pinning down visually, and the floor (rugs) and windows (curtains) are elements that need to be considered for the 'cocoon' effect to be complete.

As a painter and decorator I understand how difficult it is to get this kind of colour scheme to 'click' and create the calming, soothing, dateless 'atmosphere' that it is all about. It cannot be done from a drawing board or story board, but should grow over time, with time for reflection. Your triumph, when you get it right, will be that you have created a room that is evocative and timeless and can absorb a great deal of family memorabilia — one that is finally a special individual 'place', not a decorating 'scheme'.

BRIGHT AND BRASH The 'in your face' colour palette shown in this version of our ongoing room set is the one most likely to appeal to anyone under thirty. It owes something to vivid ethnic paint colours — Mexican, Moroccan, Indian — but more still, in its bravado, to current fashion where fluorescent colours and funky mixes of fierce, saturated primaries and secondaries put over a 'look at me' message that is fun, disconcerting and impossible to ignore. It was an absorbing challenge to put the set together, working through shades of green (skirting) and pink (frame) until the ensemble suddenly 'clicked', and it taught me a lot about handling colour at its boldest. It also gave me an insight into the sheer excitement of working with the sort of clean, unsludged hues that the work of twentieth-century colourists like Matisse, Bonnard, and more recently, Howard Hodgkin, shows being developed throughout their painting lives.

I have encountered versions of this type of colour confrontation in Greek tavernas, Mexican artefacts, Indian textiles, Goanese street scenes, always with a heightened awareness that sheer intensity of colour equals visual drama. Possessions are inevitably diminished and washed out in such a clamorous context, but for anyone who has a minimalist approach to what they own these hot and strong colour combinations can be liberating and uplifting. You can't afford a Matisse, but you can live *in* one. Not forever perhaps, on a day-to-day basis — but as a quick fix for a temporary pad inhabited in snatches, what could be more immediate, dynamic and consciousness-raising?

The beauty of the bright and brash approach is that it is done with colour, using paint, which is still the cheapest route. Your 1950s and 1960s plastics, glass and 'bits' will fall into place without a murmur.

There are designer fabrics, tiles, ceramics, etc. that fit in with this palette, but these are always relatively costly. Making your own 'patchwork' of cleverly chosen, and inexpensive, brilliantly coloured tiles is a possible solution for kitchen splashbacks and bathrooms, and one that is becoming trendy. Cheap fabrics like hessian, dyed in magnificent colours, and saris from 'sari centres' offer suitably gaudy colour mixes if you need curtains, blinds and cushions. But it is essentially the paint colours, on walls, fittings, etceteras, that will put across the 'bright and brash' story.

So how do you get the colour mix right? Any of the 'sources' mentioned above could provide a workable formula. The trick is to use colours in the right proportions and to avoid 'subtle' or 'greyed' ones like the plague. The orange of the chair and the vivid blue of our set were a safe pairing in this heightened palette. The viridian green (inspired by a Greek café) that I initially tried for the skirting looked 'dead' against these, but a lime green fired up the combination brilliantly. However, on their own, these three wild colours seemed to lack something — a counterpoint was needed. I considered and tried scarlet for the picture frame. Too obvious, and too competitive. Crimson was too dark, and purple too close to the blue wall colour. Then I remembered the chalky, hot pink of Mexican folk art. Once I had 'captured' it, mixing quinacridone violet, crimson and scarlet with white, and tried it out, my gut reaction (trust this when working with these colours) was yes, OK. But the set still needed the intense magenta and blue-green of our dyed fabrics, to 'come alive'. A real room with four walls and natural light sources will be less de-

Vivid blue walls: inspired by Matisse, this colour provides a contrasting strong background to the more vibrant colours in the details of this room.

Lime green skirting board: we needed a real lime green here to prevent dulling down the whole effect.

BRIGHT A

manding than our 'maquette' room set. And like our cotton napkins, the rogue colour that sparks it up can be small, cheap and expendable. Flowers, cushions, candles, coloured glass lamps can all supply the final 'tweak' colourwise. Although the area needed may be tiny, like the picture frame, it is important: at this intensity, success with colour is a question of balance.

Painted chair: an almost tangerine orange makes this jump out from the walls.

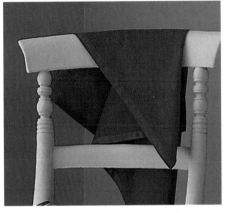

Fabrics: as with the frame, the colours in these details provide essential contrast – we used vivid Indian cottons.

Picture frame: a hot pink turned out to be the perfect counterpoint – scarlet was too competitive, and darker shades than that begin to merge with the wall. I mixed this colour with the pink of Mexican folk art in mind – with violet, crimson, scarlet and white.

75

DELICIOUS DARKNESS It is a fact that most people fight shy of darkness, especially on walls. It is a brave move to go from lightness and brightness into the powerful and enveloping statement of a dark colour, whether it be midnight blue, plum, crimson, bitter chocolate, pewter grey or, scariest of all, black. It is as drastic a one as dyeing blonde hair black — and rather more tedious to alter. Until you have tried it, it is almost impossible to visualize what a plunge into darkness will do to a room.

One, possibly unexpected, effect is to throw all the other colours into greater relief. Pictures, rugs and fabrics stand out with a new, exciting brilliance against truly dark walls. Another, more predictable, result is that the room becomes strikingly a 'place' not just a 'space', however charming. Dark walls lend 'gravitas', and a certain architectural weightiness which can be grand, as in the armoury designed by William Morris in St James's Palace, London, or as primitive as a Scandinavian loghouse. They cocoon, and in some mysterious way they make people feel safer.

Paradoxical as it may seem, some of the most vivid rooms I have seen were mainly black. In a re-creation of Sir Edwin Lutyens' study at an exhibition of his work, the plasterwork ceiling and dado were crisp white, with intense black walls between them. The floor was emerald green. Handsome pieces of polished mahogany and rosewood stood against the walls, and several portraits in gilt frames were hung against the black. The effect was sumptuous and memorable. Another black room which stays in my mind is the library at Charleston, home of the painters Vanessa Bell and Duncan Grant, two leading lights of the Bloomsbury Group. Here the overall effect was more playfully colourful: black, but distemper black (which has a soft, charcoal texture) for the main walls, enlivened by one wall of cream-painted bookcases, an old and vivid rug on the floor and Grant's own wall

paintings (a cockerel, a family dog) above and below one of the windows. These were vividly, but not crudely, painted in distemper which the couple used throughout the old farmhouse, probably because it was cheap and they could have fun with it. I particularly noticed that the ravishing garden views formed by the windows were in no way blighted by the contrast with the black room. Indeed, nature looked all the more alluring. Then, too, reaching back in time, old rooms panelled in time-blackened oak are a handsome feature of many British houses, colleges, etc. built three, four or five hundred years ago.

Dark colours 'possess' a space and set off its contents. And currently, it must be said, they are on the cutting-edge of decoration. At a recent interior decorating show, a single black room, contrasted with blonde and darker wood and black-brown-cream check fabric, stole the show from all the chintzy, pretty-to-die-for stands. It looked 'clean' (a buzz word), arresting and serious, in a way that perhaps only decorators understand. It was neither gloomy nor depressing.

I predict, sticking my neck out, that dramatically dark interiors are on the way back. Hence our last room set, which goes the whole way — to black — for walls. They are enriched, however, with a repeat stencil pattern (taken from the 'Indian Kitchen' in one of my stencil sets — see page 96) executed in a new, exciting formulation that combines graphite powder (as in pencils) with fast-drying shellac. The mix is a stencil painter's dream, drying as it hits the wall. The result over black or any truly dark shade is opulent, elegant and anything but drab — judge for your-

Stained floor: for warmth and texture, and polished to reflect the light.

Paisley walls: painted a basic matt black, but enriched with a repeated stencil pattern using a graphite-and-shellac-combination paint which catches the light and enlivens surfaces – but without changing the underlying colour.

self. Like a silk brocade, it catches the light in a fascinating way, silvery on one wall, satiny black on another. It has, for me, a charge similar to pearly glaze over white although it is at the other end of the spectrum. But with its darkness it is seriously grand. Used in a damask pattern over black walls, it would look sumptuous.

We played around with strong colour against this powerful background, but it tended to look crass, a one-liner. My feeling is that such a backcloth demands noble materials in the foreground. Thus the stained, polished boards for warmth and texture. The picture frame was a last-minute whim, inspired by the check fabric at the interior decorating show. The chair looked cheeky in matt emerald green — a brilliant colour mix, by the way (see below) — but I secretly felt that a proper mahogany chair with a proper leather seat had the quality appropriate to this finish. The photographer was all for painting the baseboard red, green or yellow (all quite

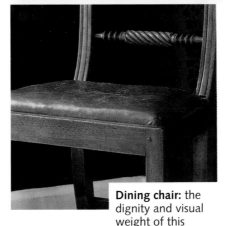

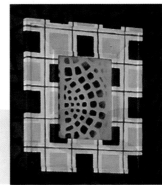

Picture frame: checks re-work the basic colours of the room but provide visual spice.

Dining chair: the dignity and visual weight of this leather-upholstered mahogany chair provided the quality this finish requires.

Skirting board: a matt, stony off-white brings useful contrast.

possible against dark walls) but by then the ancestral grandeur of our last-minute finish carried the field for me. We settled for a stony matt off-white.

It is only fair, having made such a pitch for a dark decorating palette, to answer the questions which will inevitably follow. Do dark wall colours make a room look darker? Yes, by daylight they inevitably do, although bright colours in furnishing will mitigate this. By electric light, halogens, etc. the effect is surprisingly intimate. Do they make rooms look smaller? Again yes, compared with transparent finishes, for instance, but they can give them a new impressiveness. Dark colours are great for studies, dressing rooms (how grand can we get?) and small spaces which aspire to look luxurious and will mainly be seen by artificial light. A black or chocolate dining room, properly handled, could look superb. Finally, dark colours flatter people — a point to bear in mind.

COLOUR: THE RAW MATERIALS

When commercial paint ranges offer as many as 2000 different shades you may wonder what point there is in attempting to mix your own. Well, believe it or not, you may not find the very colour you want among 2000 colour chips. But with a little 'tweaking' — a dollop of raw umber, a squeeze of purple-red, whatever — you can get it exactly right. If transparent colour (see page 38) tempts you it is very often easier to hit on the right shade by tinting your own, as pre-tinted commercial ranges tend to be limited. But the best reason to get wised up about colour-mixing is that it gives you control of the situation. Instead of breakneck dashes to the DIY shed to swap the colour that looked great on the paint card, but lurid on the wall, you simply reach for your box of tricks — your tinting agents — add a bit of this and that, mix and test, and the problem is solved. Knowing that you can make any paint or paint effect work for you will instil confidence, save money and encourage you to become creative about decorating — a decorative artist rather than a mere house painter.

TINTING AGENTS

The first step is to familiarize yourself with the different tinting agents on offer. These are the colour-mixer's tools and, as a browse around any good artists' supplier will demonstrate, they come in a bewildering variety of types, names and colours. Tinting agents offer pigment in a highly concentrated form, commonly in either an oil or acrylic base. Artist's quality paints are the most expensive but their colours tend to be truer and more intense than the cheaper student ranges. Other tinting agents include dry pigments, which come in powder form, and universal stainers sold in large tubes. They all have their pros and cons and these are discussed in more detail below. But the most important fact to take on board if you are using them to tint commercial paints, rather than 'straight' as fine artists do, is that the tinting agent you choose must be compatible with the type of paint, glaze or varnish you plan to use. Broadly speaking, most commercial paints are either oil- or water-based, with water-based emulsion paints dominating the domestic market. The rule here is Like with Like. Oil-bound pigments (artist's oil colours) are used to tint oil-based products, artist's acrylic colours for water-based ones. Dry pigments and universal stainers can be used to tint both. Acrylic colours differ from traditional watercolours in that they are insoluble once dry — they will not wash off. You can be sure that any product featuring the word acrylic (primer, glaze and varnish as well as artist's paints) will be fast drying, permanent, and require brushes to be cleaned as soon as possible in warm water. Checking the manufacturer's printed instructions about brush-cleaning is the clincher if you are in doubt about which family the product belongs to. Alkyds, for instance, which some people confuse with acrylics, specify white spirit for cleaning brushes because they are oil-based.

There is no need to invest in a huge range of tinting agents. One colour-mixer of the old school proudly informed me that he could supply any colour required from a mere half-dozen universal stainers, i.e. the three primaries (red, blue and yellow), plus black, raw umber and either burnt sienna or lemon yellow. I remain a little doubtful about this claim, but it is true that a wide range of colours can be produced from a restricted palette by clever intermixing. Finding out what you can create from a limited selection of tinting agents is a sensible, thrifty discipline and a challenge for beginners.

Artist's oil colours Sold in tubes, these are intensely pigmented and very pure and come in a wide range of superior, refined colours which are readily dissolved in white spirit prior to mixing into oil-bound products, including alkyds. They can be used to tint oil-based eggshell, flat or gloss paints, and also transparent oil glaze and polyurethane varnishes. Although not as powerful as pure pigments or universal stainers, oil colours are relatively expensive; some categories cost more than others because of rarity of pigment or complexity of manufacture. Terebine driers can be added to mixed paints, following instructions, to speed up their drying time. White spirit cleans up.

Artist's acrylic colours Sold in tubes, plastic jars and bottles, these come in a good colour range including fluorescent colours and metallics. They are fast drying — and permanent when dry — so re-cap containers and wash brushes out promptly. Dissolve in water and use to tint water-based products including emulsion paints, acrylic scumble (glaze) and varnish. Acrylics are also useful for stencilling, or delicate applied decoration; add Flow Enhancer for fluidity and to retard drying. Beware of overloading paints with acrylic tinting colours — if you do they can misbehave; start with a shelf colour close to what you want. Water cleans up.

Universal stainers Sold in fat tubes, their colour range limited and somewhat crude, but they are powerful as tints. They can be used with oil-based (dissolve first in white spirit), water-based (dissolve first in water) and other paint products — a great advantage. Relatively inexpensive, stainers are widely available in DIY sheds as well as from local paint shops. A sensible buy for beginners. Intermixable.

Dry powder pigments Usually sold in glass jars, through artists' suppliers, or in bulk via specialist firms, these are the purest form of pigment available, and therefore relatively expensive but powerful. They can be used to tint both oil- (dissolve first in white spirit) and water-based (dissolve first in water) products, and have the further advantage that they will not interfere with paint chemistry. Pigments must be well soaked and thoroughly dissolved before use — one tiny undissolved grain can land up as big streak of colour on the wall. Ideal tinting agents for limewash and fresco, and traditionally used to colour soft distemper, they can also be used (dissolved first in methylated spirits) to colour shellac for home-made lacquer. Good artists' suppliers stock a wide colour range; earth colours are usually the cheapest. Avoid playschool-type powder pigments which contain extenders.

Sample jars Many commercial manufacturers offer small colour samples which can, of course, be used to tint or modify a shelf-paint colour. Follow the Like with Like rule; this is rarely a problem since almost all of these today will be water-based acrylics. Using samples is not the most economical way to tint, but it is convenient and quick. It makes sense to choose the deepest shade of your colour on offer, as this will give more colour for less paint. A decorative painter's money saving tip is to buy the darkest colour on a shade card and mix it with cheaper white emulsion to arrive at the desired mid- or pale tone.

This is by no means a complete list of possible tinting agents. However, it covers the most reliable and versatile ones commonly used by professionals, who rarely apply an off-the-shelf paint as it comes, but 'tweak' the colour to make it brighter, softer, more subtle or closer to a historic one — or to create a shade that fulfils the client's brief to match a fabric, carpet, etc.

MIXING YOUR OWN COLOURS

Follow the example of professional decorative painters and start by tinting small quantities of paint, making a note of colours used, and in roughly what proportion. Then, when you have your desired colour you can replicate the formula on a larger scale. This is the bit that invariably makes beginners anxious because they find it hard to believe that they will be able to match several litres of paint exactly to their sample, just as they worry about running out of a tinted paint before the job is finished. The answer is that matching a shade is easier than you might suppose, providing you know what tinting colours you used and roughly how much of each. And don't worry if you haven't prepared enough paint. Colour-mixing is not an exact science. If it is any comfort, a slight variation in the final colour (so long as it doesn't happen mid-wall) will be undetectable to all but a trained eye.

1 Dissolve your tinting agent in just enough of the appropriate solvent to make a fluid mixture. Use a stiff-bristled fitch to mash it up thoroughly in the solvent. Standard paint brushes are not small and precise enough for this job. It is difficult to determine the amount of tinting solution you will need when you repeat the formula on a larger scale, so make a note of the proportion of tinting agent to solvent in case you need to make up more of the mixture. If you are using several colours in a solution it is best to keep their dissolved tints separate.

2 Add the tinted mixture to a spoonful or two of paint — just enough to cover a sample card and still have a 'wet sample' to consult. When you have the shade you want, make a note of the colour or colours and the rough proportions in which they were used. Keep your sample in a screwtop jar and store any surplus tinted solutions in airtight jars.

3 Repeat the process with the required quantity of paint. If you are using more than one can of paint it may be helpful to tip them into a large bucket — you can pour a manageable quantity into a paint kettle or can when you start work. Add the tinting solutions gradually to your base paint in approximately the proportions noted. Stir very thoroughly as you do this.

Use a long-handled wooden spoon rather than a stick and stir for longer than seems necessary. Test the colour on paper after each addition and compare it with your control swatch. You can use a hair drier to speed up drying. Provided you proceed slowly, mix well and test regularly, you are bound to get there in the end.

Finally, some tips to bear in mind:

■ Start by 'tweaking' an existing paint colour. This is easier, quicker and cheaper than starting from white unless you want a very light pastel colour. Always mix dark colours from a shade close to the one you are aiming at.

■ If you overdo the final colour, lighten it by buying and adding more of the off-the-shelf paint colour. A sample size may be all you need.

■ If your hand slips and you add too much of one colour so that the formula is unbalanced, add another can of the off-the-shelf paint, mix well and add more of the other tinting colours.

■ Keep your colour-mixing notes and wet sample and test card in case you want to touch up, repaint or simply repeat a successful colour. Label everything clearly.

■ When you are tinting a glaze or wash to go over a paint colour, test the tint on a board painted with the same base colour.

■ Don't add too much solvent to your tinting agent before mixing. If you do, your paint will become too thin to cover well.

A COLOUR-MIXER'S WORKBOX

I recommend a few basics to have to hand when mixing your own colours. You can add to these over time.

TOOLS AND EQUIPMENT

■ artist's long-handled fitch (the firm, stiff bristles will break up the tinting media, rather than absorbing them as happens with a standard paint brush)
■ waxed paper plates (as mixing palettes)
■ plastic buckets or paint kettles, glass jars with lids (for mixing and storing)
■ white paper or card (for testing colours)
■ artist's small brushes (for testers)
■ solvents: water, white spirit, methylated spirits (or denatured alcohol)
■ hair dryer
■ optional: pestle and mortar or a decorator's muller (to grind pigment finely)

BASIC TINTING COLOURS

■ Universal stainers in red, blue, yellow, raw umber, black and white make up a versatile basic palette which will give a wide colour range in both oil and water-based media.
■ Add missing 'undertones' (blue, red, green, yellow, cerulean) as the need arises.
■ Raw umber is useful for softening most colours, and a safer way to deaden them than using black, which must always be used sparingly and gradually.

SOURCES AND SUPPLIERS

Atlantis European Ltd
146 Brick Lane
London E1 6RU
tel (0171) 377 8855
fax (0171) 377 8850
Art and conservation
supplies

Auro Organic Paints
White Horse House
Ashdon, nr Saffron
    Walden
Essex CB10 2ET
tel (01799) 584888
fax (01799) 584887
Mail order

Biofa Natural Paints
5 School Road
Kidlington
Oxford OX5 2HB
tel (018675) 4964
Environmentally sound
products

J.W. Bollom
121 South Liberty Lane
Ashton Vale, Bristol
tel (01179) 665151
Glazes, varnishes,
tinting colours and
paints

Brodie & Middleton
    Ltd
68 Drury Lane
London WC2
tel (0171) 836 3289
Dry pigments

H.J. Chard & Son Ltd
Albert Road
Bristol BS2 0XS
tel (01179) 777681
fax (01179) 719802
Mail order specialists in
limewashing

Cole & Son (Wallpapers)
    Ltd
144 Offord Road
London N1 1NS
tel (0171) 607 4288
Hand-blocked
wallpapers, fabrics and
special paint colours;
mail order

Colourman Paints
Stockingate
Cotton Clanford, Staffs
tel (01785) 282799
Historic paints and
supplies

Cornelissen & Son Ltd
105 Great Russell Street
London WC1B 3RY
tel (0171) 636 1045
fax (0171) 636 3655
Artist's supplies, and
mail order

Craig & Rose plc
172 Leith Walk
Edinburgh EH6 5ER
tel (0131) 554 1131
Old-established paint
firm, with very extensive
ranges. Call for nearest
supplier

Falkiner Fine Papers Ltd
76 Southampton Row
London WC1B 4AR
tel (0171) 831 1151
Specialist papers

A.P. Fitzpatrick
1 Barnabas Studios
10-22 Barnabas Road
London E9 5SB
tel 0181 985 7865
fax 0181 985 7659

Hirst Conservation
Materials Ltd
Laughton, nr Sleaford
Lincolnshire NG34 0HE
tel (01529) 497517
fax (01529) 497518
Traditional paint
specialists

Liz and Bruce Induni
11 Park Road
Swanage, Dorset BH19
    2AA
tel (01924 423274)
Limewash, distemper
and pigments

Masons Mortar
61-67 Trafalgar Lane
Edinburgh EH6 4DQ
tel (0131) 555 0503
Lime and conservation
materials; mail order

Nutshell Natural Paints
10 High Street, Totnes
Devon TQ9 5RY
tel (01803) 867770
mail order:
Newtake
Staverton, Devon
TQ9 6PE
tel (01803) 762329

Papers and Paints
4 Park Walk
London SW10 0AD
tel (0171) 352 8626
Historic paints, matched
glazes, stencils; mail
order

E. Ploton (Sundries) Ltd
273 Archway Road
London N6 5AA
tel (0181) 348 0315
Artist's materials; mail
order

Putnams
34 Somali Road
London NW2 3RL
tel (0171) 431 2935
fax (0171) 794 2586
Very good for bright
colours; specialists in
Mediterranean colours.
Mail order

J.H. Ratcliffe & Co.
    (Paints) Ltd
135A Linekar Street
Southport PR8 5DF
tel (O1704) 37999
Good for equipment and
glazes; call for mail order
and stockists

George Rowney & Co.
    Ltd
12 Percy Street
London W1A 2BP
tel (0171) 636 8241
Famous artist's
materials supplier, with
wide range of colour
supplies; mail order

Jane Schofield
Lewdon Farm
Black Dog
Crediton, Devon
EX17 4QQ
tel (01884) 861181
Lime and conservation
materials; mail order

Stuart R. Stevenson
68 Clerkenwell Road
London EC1M 5QA
tel (0171) 253 1693
fax (0171) 490 0451
Artist's materials; mail
order

Winsor & Newton
Whitefriars Avenue
Wealdstone, Harrow
HA3 5RH
tel (0181) 427 4343)
Head office; call for local
stockists of these world-
famous artist's supplies

UNITED STATES

Home Depot
2727 Paces Serry Road
    NW
Atlanta, GA 30339
tel (404) 433 8211
call (800) 553 3199 for
store nearest you

Janovic/Plaza Inc.
30-35 Thomson Avenue
Long Island City, NY
11101
tel (718) 392 3999
Call for branches of this
decorating supplies chain

Donald Kaufman Color
410 West 13th Street,
    2nd floor
New York, NY 10014
tel (212) 243 2766
fax (212) 929 9816
catalogue and mail order:
114 West Palisade
    Avenue
Englewood, NJ 07631
tel (201) 568 2226
Good range of mixed
colours

Livos Plant Chemistry
1365 Rufina Circle
Santa Fe, NM 87501
tel (505) 438 3448
fax (505) 438 0199
Specialists in natural
paints and varnishes

Benjamin Moore & Co.
51 Chestnut Bridge Road
Montvale, NJ 07645
tel (201) 573 9600
fax (201) 573 0046
Call (800) 826 2623 for
local stockists
Widely-stocked range of
paints, varnishes, stains
etc.

New England Resins and
Pigments Corporation
316 New Boston Street
Woburn, MA 01801
tel (617) 935 8910
fax (617) 933 4417

Pearl Paint
308 Canal Street
New York, NY 10013
tel (212) 431 7932

The Stulb Company
East Allen & North
Graham Streets
P.O. Box 597
Allentown,
PA 18105-4273
tel (215) 433 4273
fax (215) 433 6116
Historic paint collection
available by mail order

CANADA

Artist Emporium Ltd
106-1135 64th Avenue
SE , Calgary, Alberta
T2H 2I7
tel (403) 255 2090 /
(800) 661 8341
fax (403) 255 8780 /
(800) 263 2329
Full range of artist's
supplies

Barnes Artists Supply
132-10th Street NW
Calgary, Alberta
T2N 1V3
tel (403) 283 2288

Gemst Inc.
5380 Sherbrooke West
Montreal, Quebec
H4A 1V6
tel (514) 488 5104
fax (514) 488 9343
Colour supplies and
media

Maiwa Handprints
6-1666 Johnston Street
Granville Island
Vancouver
British Columbia V6H
3S2
tel (604) 669 3939
fax (604) 669 0609
Specialist decorating
supplies and equipment

Benjamin Moore & Co.
139 Mulock Avenue
Toronto, Ontario
M6N 1G9
tel (416) 766 1173
fax (416) 766 9677
Widely-stocked range of
paints, varnishes, stains
etc.

Omer DeSerres
334 Ste-Catherine East
Montreal, Quebec
H2X 1L7
tel (514) 842 6637
fax (514) 842 1413
Wide range of colour
supplies

Reid's Art Materials Ltd
5847 Victoria Drive
Vancouver, British
Columbia V5P 3W5
tel (604) 321 9615
fax (604) 324 7343

Sheffield Bronze Inc.
710 Ormont Drive
Weston, Ontario
M9L 2Y5
tel (416) 749 8800
fax (416) 749 8659
Extensive range of
metallic colour supplies,
plus equipment

Societé Internationale
Canadienne Tobgi Inc.
2301 Guénette Street
Montreal, Québec
H4R 2E9
tel (514) 745 1551
fax (514) 745 1552
Fine art and designer
paints

Stevenson DL & Son
Artist's Colour
Manufacturing Co. Ltd
1420 Warden Avenue
Scarborough, Ontario
M1R 5A3
tel (416) 755 7795
fax (416) 755 5895

Talens C.A.C. Inc.
2 Waterman Street
St Lambert, Quibec
J4P 1RB
tel (514) 672 9931
fax (514) 672 4754
Paints etc.

AUSTRALASIA

Bristol Decorator Centre
76 Oatley Court
Belconnen, ACT 2617
Australia

Country Colours
10 Broadway
New Market,
New Zealand
tel (03) 65 8234

Janet's Art Supplies
143-145 Victoria Avenue
Chatswood, NSW 2067
Australia
tel (02) 9417 8572
fax (02) 9417 7617

Oxford Art Supplies Pty
Ltd
221-223 Oxford Street
Darlinghurst, NSW 2010
Australia
tel (02) 9360 4066
fax (02) 9360 3461

Peter Sudich Discount
Art Supplies
155 Katoomba Street
Katoomba, NSW 2780
Australia
tel (047) 82 2866
fax (047) 82 1318

Porter's Paints
11 Albion Way
Surry Hills, NSW 2010
Australia
tel (02) 9281 2413
fax (02) 9281 5724

592 Willoughby Road
Willoughby, NSW 2062
tel (02) 9958 0753

Randwick Art and Craft
Supplies
203 Avoca Street
Randwick, NSW 2031
tel (02) 9398 3375

PAINT MAGIC SHOPS

Paint Magic offers a complete range of decorative paints, traditional ingredients, brushes, stencils and books. Each branch also offers weekly courses in decorative paint techniques.

PAINT MAGIC
MAIL ORDER
79 Shepperton Road
Islington, London
N1 3DF
United Kingdom
tel (0171) 226 4420
fax (0171) 226 7760

UNITED KINGDOM

PAINT MAGIC
ARUNDEL
26 The High Street
Arundel, West Sussex
BN18 9AB
tel (01903) 883653
fax (01903) 884367

PAINT MAGIC
BELFAST
59 The High Street
Holywood, County
Down BT18 9AQ
tel (01232) 421881
fax (01232) 421823

PAINT MAGIC
GUILDFORD
3 Chapel Street
Guildford, Surrey
GU1 3UH
tel (01483) 306072

PAINT MAGIC
ISLINGTON
34 Cross Street
Islington, London
N1 2BG
tel (0171) 359 4441
fax (0171) 359 1833

PAINT MAGIC
NOTTING HILL
5 Elgin Crescent
Notting Hill Gate,
London W11 2JA
tel (0171) 792 8012
fax (0171) 727 0207

PAINT MAGIC
RICHMOND
116 Sheen Road
Richmond, Surrey
TW9 1UR
tel (0181) 940 9799
fax (0181) 332 7503

UNITED STATES

Paint Magic products are stocked by Pottery Barn branches across the United States. For details of your nearest stockist, call Pottery Barn customer service (800) 922 9934, or write to:

POTTERY BARN
MAIL ORDER
DEPARTMENT
P.O. Box 7044
San Francisco, CA
94120-7044
tel (415) 983 9887

CANADA

PAINT MAGIC
CALGARY
101, 1019 # 17th Avenue
SW Calgary, Alberta
T2T 0A7
tel (403) 245 6866
fax (403) 244 2471

ISRAEL

PAINT MAGIC
TEL AVIV
255 Dijengoff Street
Tel Aviv 63117
tel (972) 3605 2476
fax (972) 3544 5710

SINGAPORE

PAINT MAGIC
SINGAPORE
Seik Yee Paint Shop
30 Watten Rise
Singapore 1128
tel (65) 463 1982
fax (65) 463 1982

FURTHER DETAILS

There are more Paint Magic shops opening worldwide in the near future. Please call or write for our catalogue, price list, Design and Decoration Service and details of the latest shop to open near you.

PAINT MAGIC
HEAD OFFICE
77 Shepperton Road
Islington, London
N1 3DF
United Kingdom
tel (44) (0)171 354 9696
fax (44) (0)171 226 7760

Series Origination: Jocasta Innes
Text and Research: Jocasta Innes

Design: Hammond Hammond

Original Photography:
Marie-Louise Avery, Sue Baker
Project Manager: Sarah Curran
Assistants: Sammy Dent, Thandi
McPherson, Tim Tari
Senior Commissioning Editor for
Boxtree/Macmillan: Gordon Scott Wise
Editor: Tessa Clark

First published 1997 by Macmillan
an imprint of Macmillan Publishers Ltd
25 Eccleston Place, London SW1W 9NF
and Basingstoke

Associated companies throughout the
world

ISBN 0 333 71440 7

9 8 7 6 5 4 3 2

A CIP catalogue record for this book is
available from the British Library

ACKNOWLEDGEMENTS
Grateful thanks to the designer Emily
Readett-Bayley for permission to
photograph her house, which is featured on
the front jacket, and to Paint Magic Islington
for the display featured on page 62.
The 'paisley' stencil pattern featured on page
79 is taken from the 'Indian Kitchen' in the
Paintability Patterns of the World Collection.

PICTURE CREDITS
Marie-Louise Avery 2, 12, 16, 23, 31, 43/44,
82; Sue Baker 1 (except inside right), 3
(bottom), 14-15, 19, 20, 21, 25, 28-9, 33,
34, 36-7, 38-9, 41, 42, 46-7, 49, 50-1, 54-5,
57, 58-9, 60-1, 62, 65, 66-7, 68-9, 70, 72-3,
74-5, 76, 78-9, 80-1, 87 (bottom); Jocasta
Innes 3 (top); Paint Magic 1 (inside right),
87 (top), 90, 92, 95

Scans and colour repro by Speedscan Ltd.

Printed in Italy by New Interlitho S.P.A. – Milan